D1017175

moments of
SERENITY

ESME FIELDING

summersdale

MOMENTS OF SERENITY

Copyright © Summersdale Publishers Ltd, 2014

Text contributed by Alexa Ball

All images © Shutterstock

Summersdale Publishers Ltd
46 West Street
Chichester
West Sussex
PO19 1RP
UK

www.summersdale.com

Printed and bound in China

ISBN: 978-1-84953-518-2

Substantial discounts on bulk quantities of Summersdale books are available to corporations, professional associations and other organisations. For details contact Nicky Douglas by telephone: +44 (0) 1243 756902, fax: +44 (0) 1243 786300 or email: nicky@summersdale.com.

INTRODUCTION

Taking time out for quiet, calm and relaxation is vital to our wellbeing, allowing us to disconnect from the noise of today's hectic world of fast food, high-speed Internet and constant connectedness. Finding peace and tranquillity in our day-to-day lives can be as simple as enjoying a gentle stroll or a warm bath, and helps us to see the magic and wonder in the world around us without judgement or stress. Let this book guide you from morning to night, showing how you can bring small but beautiful moments of serenity to each and every day.

Start your day by

STRETCHING,

remembering to breathe deeply.

RELEASE TENSION

both in body and soul and

BEGIN THE DAY

in a state of inner peace.

Today, choose to

RADIATE POSITIVITY

and

PEACEFULNESS

in all you do.

Before beginning your day,

TAKE THREE DEEP BREATHS,

allowing the air to open your chest.

LENGTHEN YOUR SPINE

and leave you feeling centred

AND PREPARED.

Rise early today to gaze at the

NATURE OUTSIDE

your window, whether in sunshine,

RAIN OR SNOW.

Think of the possibilities of

THE DAY AHEAD,

and choose to

PAINT YOUR CANVAS

with peace and serenity.

Use single words to describe

YOUR EMOTIONS,

making it simpler for you to

ADDRESS THEM

and restore

INNER PEACE.

Facial expressions are your

WINDOW TO THE WORLD;

a gentle smile on your face

BRINGS INNER CALM

and outward joy to the day.

Dress in soft fabrics in

GENTLE COLOURS

to become your own

IMAGE OF SERENITY.

Leave notes around your space reminding you to

'BREATHE' AND 'BE CALM'.

Take a moment to pause and

CENTRE YOURSELF

whenever you spot them.

Seek tranquillity
IN NATURE,
in the greens of the leaves and the
EARTHY BROWNS
of the trunks.
CENTRE YOURSELF
with the balance of
YOUR SURROUNDINGS.

Take joy in the people and

THINGS AROUND YOU.

Seek to expand your

HEART AND MIND,

not your possessions.

Your affirmation for today

IS TO WHISPER

quietly to yourself,

'I AM AT PEACE.'

Plan ahead.

USE A CALENDAR

as a visual aid to know

WHAT'S COMING NEXT,

and make sure to leave

ROOM FOR RELAXING.

Collect pictures or postcards
THAT INSPIRE A FEELING
of serenity, and place them
ON YOUR DESK
or on the fridge to use when
YOU NEED INSPIRATION.

Set aside time each month for
YOUR FAVOURITE
relaxing activity, such as sitting by a
REAL LOG FIRE
or enjoying a leisurely meal
WITH FRIENDS.

Fill your mind with

POSITIVE PHRASES,

inspirational ideas and

AFFIRMATIONS.

Use these to

REPLACE ANY NEGATIVE

thoughts that arise during the day.

Open your windows and let

NATURAL LIGHT

brighten your space, allowing

THE RADIANCE

of the sun to soak

INTO YOUR SKIN.

Listen to slow, gentle music and

CLOSE YOUR EYES.

Let the notes wash over you,

FILLING YOUR MIND,

body and soul with serenity.

Today, be especially
AWARE OF YOUR BODY.
Release any tension with
DEEP BREATHS,
and focus on
MOVING SLOWLY,
deliberately and calmly.

Take art supplies to

A QUIET PLACE

in the woods. Use slow, flowing

BRUSH STROKES

and free, curving pencil lines to

RELEASE TENSION

and foster mental peace.

Speak clearly and concisely and

SAY WHAT YOU MEAN

to avoid cluttering conversation.

SIMPLICITY

is the sister of serenity.

Find a gently moving

STREAM OR FOUNTAIN

to sit beside, allowing

THE CONSTANT SOUND

to replace your thoughts and

RESTORE YOUR CALM.

Walking gives you

AN OUTLET

for your energy, and a way to

ENJOY THE WORLD

around you. Let your feet and

MIND WANDER.

Enjoy several minutes of quiet
'YOU TIME'
each day, allowing you to
SLOW THE WORLD
to your own pace and refocus
YOUR ENERGY.

A clear home is

A CLEAR MIND.

Clean and organise the

SPACES AROUND YOU

to escape the stress of mess.

Name your intent.
HAVING A CLEAR GOAL,
be it abstract or exact,
BRINGS MEANING
to your actions.

When it's raining,

INSTEAD OF LETTING

it get you down, think of all

THE GOOD THINGS

that come from the rain –

FRESH FLOWERS

and maybe even a rainbow.

Choose an image that
REPRESENTS SERENITY
for you, such as a
BLOOMING FLOWER
or an empty beach.
VISUALISE IT
whenever you need
A FEW MOMENTS
to yourself during the day.

Allow time to
FULLY ENJOY MEALS
without rushing.
RELISH EACH BITE,
so that you finish feeling
SATISFIED AND FULFILLED.

Today write down ten

'HAPPINESS NUGGETS',

or moments throughout the day

THAT BRING YOU JOY.

Remember that each and every

JOYFUL INSTANCE

is significant.

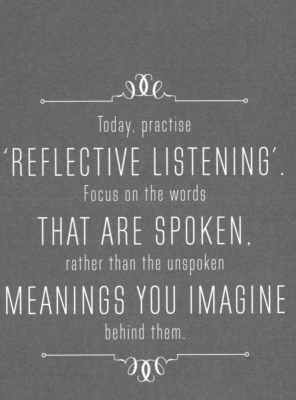

Today, practise
'REFLECTIVE LISTENING'.
Focus on the words
THAT ARE SPOKEN,
rather than the unspoken
MEANINGS YOU IMAGINE
behind them.

Today, take a walk
WITHOUT YOUR PHONE
or music player,
ENJOYING SIGHTS
and sounds with new clarity, and
WITHOUT DISTRACTION.

Be aware of

NEGATIVE PHRASES

you use, and replace them with

WORDS OF KINDNESS,

love and peace.

Today, take a moment before reacting.

BREATHE DEEPLY,

count to ten, and know that

YOU HAVE A CHOICE

in how to respond.

Past and future are insignificant compared

TO THE PRESENT.

Find a quiet place to sit comfortably

AND CENTRE YOURSELF

in the here and now.

Remember to

FOCUS YOUR ENERGY

on areas where you can

MAKE A DIFFERENCE.

Maintain your inner peace

IN TIMES OF TURMOIL

and change.

Remember: good things take time.
BUT, STEP BY STEP,
your journey will always
TAKE YOU WHERE
you need to be.

Once you have made a decision,

HAVE CONVICTION

and believe in your own capabilities.

THE ROADS TO CONFIDENCE

and calm are intertwined

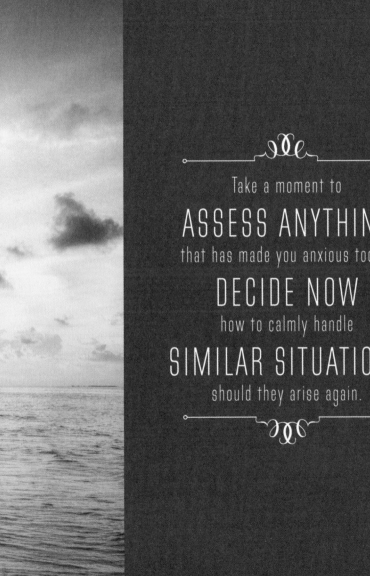

Take a moment to
ASSESS ANYTHING
that has made you anxious today.
DECIDE NOW
how to calmly handle
SIMILAR SITUATIONS
should they arise again.

Attend to each moment

AS IT HAPPENS,

experiencing the day

ONE STEP AT A TIME.

Focus on filling each

INDIVIDUAL MOMENT

with serenity.

Be sure to say 'thank you'
IN YOUR THOUGHTS
throughout the day, expanding
YOUR GRATITUDE
to include the ordinary as well as
THE EXTRAORDINARY.

Keep your inner peace strong
AND FOCUS
on cultivating serenity from within.
THE UNIVERSE
is a noisy place – it's up to you to
FIND A PATH
through the confusion of life.

Bubble baths are a great way
TO UNWIND.
Light a candle and play some
RELAXING MUSIC;
let your worries
FLOAT AWAY.

At the end of your day,
TAKE A PEACEFUL MOMENT
to close your eyes and focus
ON YOUR BREATHING.
Let go of your worries and enjoy
BEING IN THE MOMENT.

Keeping a journal of
YOUR THOUGHTS
can give you a channel to
EXPEL NEGATIVE ENERGY
and resolve the day's issues
IN YOUR MIND
before you sleep.

Dab a few drops of

LAVENDER OIL

on a handkerchief and place it

UNDER YOUR PILLOW;

let the calming aroma

HELP YOU DRIFT OFF

into a deep, restful sleep.

Meditation is a great way to

CLEAR THE COBWEBS

of the day and return to

YOUR EQUILIBRIUM.

Try it for five minutes every night to

START THE NEXT DAY

feeling calm and refreshed.

If you're interested in finding out more about our books,
find us on Facebook at Summersdale Publishers
and follow us on Twitter at @Summersdale.

www.summersdale.com